READ TO REACH

1

NE_Build & Grow

TOUR OF A UNIT

Step 1 : Before Reading

Before reading, students have the opportunity to predict the text and activate schema.

- A captivating photo and a semantic map encourage students to actively predict the text.

- **Vocabularies** are introduced and let students get ready for the text.

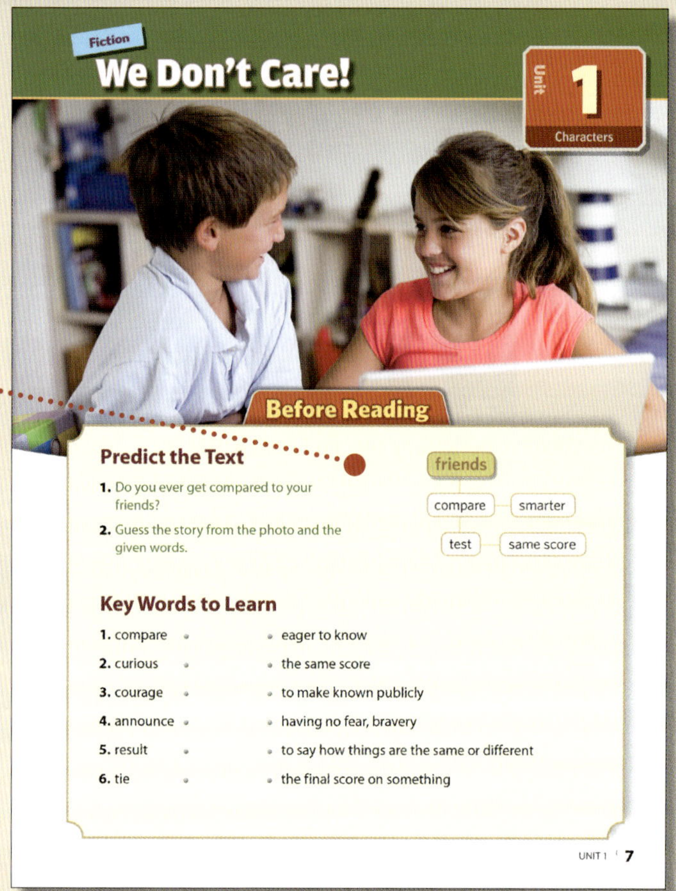

Step 2 : Reading

While reading, students are fostered to use reading skills and strategies to get the gist of the selection effectively.

- Focused reading skills are introduced with a concise definition and a chart.

- A high interest reading selection is presented and helps students improve their reading skills.

- **Text Talk** enables students to interact with the reading selection.

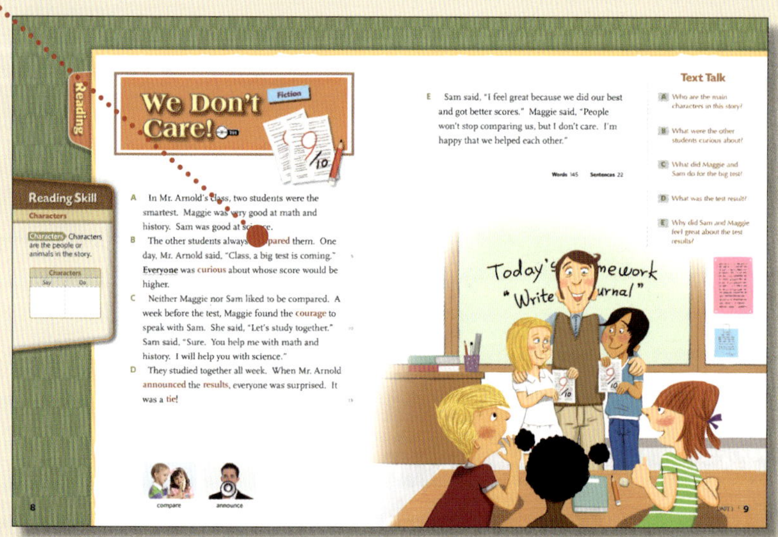

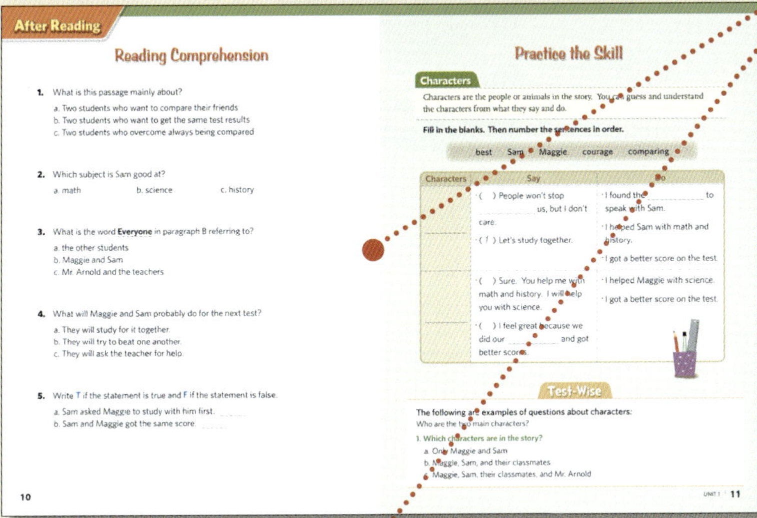

After reading, a variety of activities ensures the understanding of what the students have read with a particular focus on using the targeted reading skills and strategies.

- **Reading Comprehension** questions confirm students' understanding of the main idea, details, inferences, vocabularies, and etc.

- **Practice the Skill** offers a detailed explanation of each reading skill. A visualized graphic organizer leads students to apply the previously learned reading skill to the reading selection.

- **Test Wise** prepares students to be successful at standard tests.

- **Focus on Summarizing** builds students' summarizing skills which is one of the fundamental learning skills for all subjects. It also contributes to raise students' semantic and structural awareness of the English language.

- **Critical Thinking** challenges students to reflect on the reading selection in various ways.

Branch Out

CONTENTS

Reading Skills for Read to Reach 1

Characters

Characters are the people or animals in the story. You can guess and understand the characters from what they say and do.

Story Structure

The setting tells when and where the story takes place. The plot is the order of events.

Main Idea & Details

The topic is what the story is about. The main idea is the most important idea about the topic. Details are information that supports the main idea.

Compare & Contrast

Comparing is telling how things are alike. Contrasting is telling how things are different.

Sequence

The sequence is the order of events in the story. To identify the order, we can use time signal words.

Cause & Effect

A cause is why something happens. An effect is the result.

Fiction

We Don't Care!

Unit 1
Characters

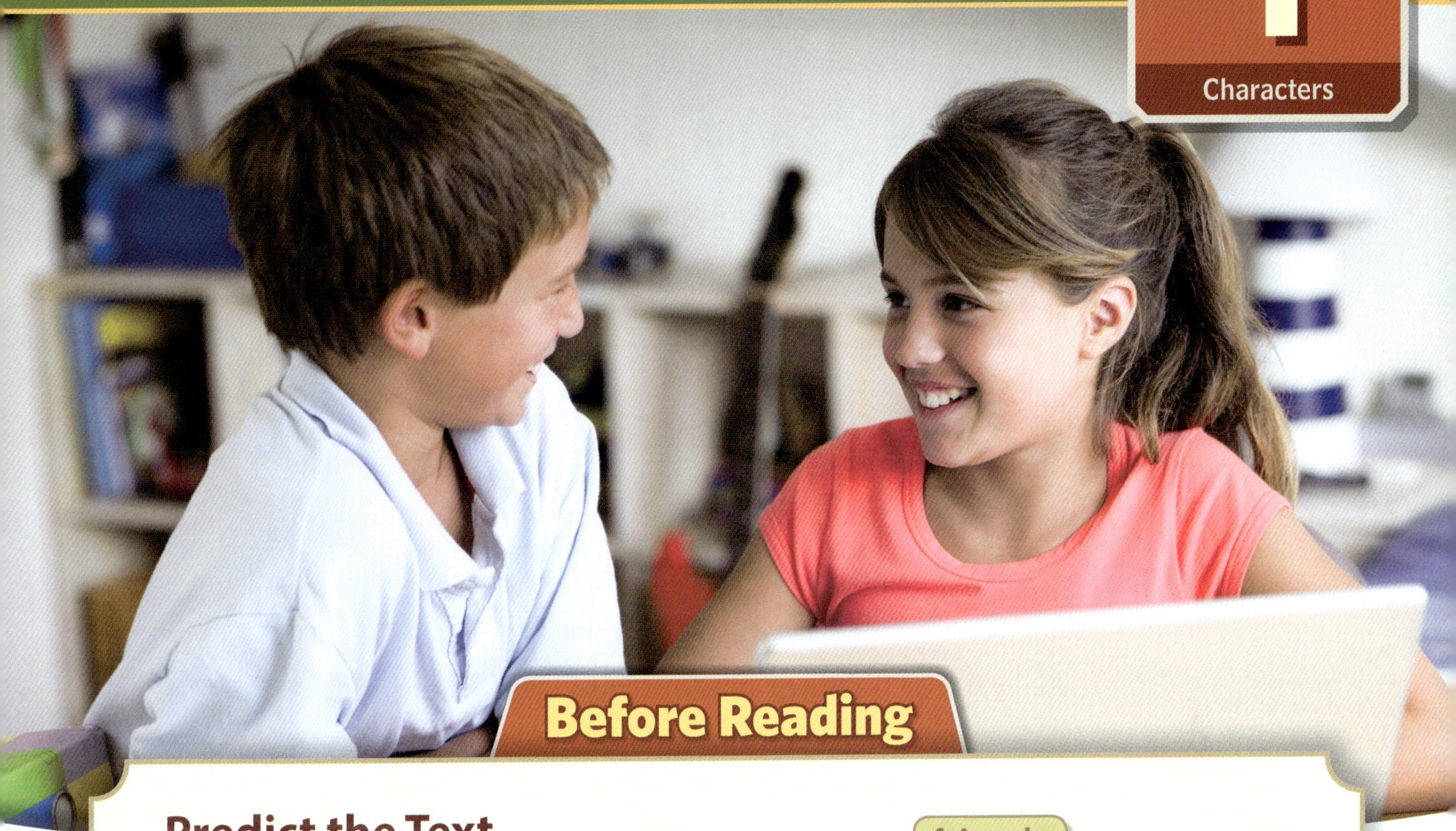

Before Reading

Predict the Text

1. Do you ever get compared to your friends?
2. Guess the story from the photo and the given words.

friends
compare — smarter
test — same score

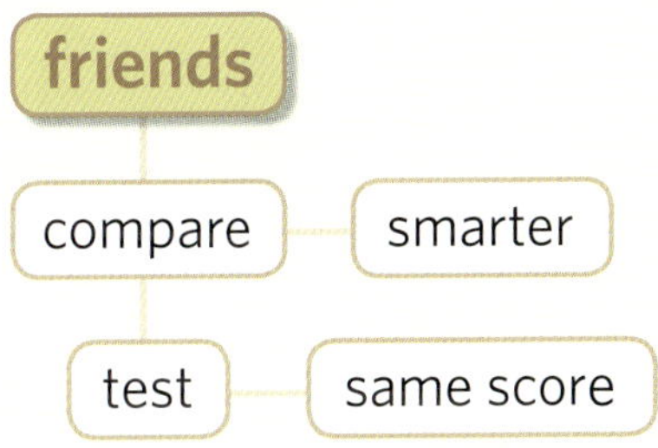

Key Words to Learn

1. compare	eager to know
2. curious	the same score
3. courage	to make known publicly
4. announce	having no fear, bravery
5. result	to say how things are the same or different
6. tie	the final score on something

We Don't Care!  T01

Fiction

Reading Skill

Characters

Characters Characters are the people or animals in the story.

Characters	
Say	Do

A In Mr. Arnold's class, two students were the smartest. Maggie was very good at math and history. Sam was good at science.

B The other students always **compared** them. One day, Mr. Arnold said, "Class, a big test is coming." **Everyone** was **curious** about whose score would be higher.

C Neither Maggie nor Sam liked to be compared. A week before the test, Maggie found the **courage** to speak with Sam. She said, "Let's study together." Sam said, "Sure. You help me with math and history. I will help you with science."

D They studied together all week. When Mr. Arnold **announced** the **results**, everyone was surprised. It was a **tie**!

5

10

15

compare

announce

E   Sam said, "I feel great because we did our best and got better scores." Maggie said, "People won't stop comparing us, but I don't care. I'm happy that we helped each other."

Words 145   **Sentences** 22

A Who are the main characters in this story?

B What were the other students curious about?

C What did Maggie and Sam do for the big test?

D What was the test result?

E Why did Sam and Maggie feel great about the test results?

Reading Comprehension

1. What is this passage mainly about?

    a. Two students who want to compare their friends
    b. Two students who want to get the same test results
    c. Two students who overcome always being compared

2. Which subject is Sam good at?

    a. math   b. science   c. history

3. What is the word **Everyone** in paragraph B referring to?

    a. The other students
    b. Maggie and Sam
    c. Mr. Arnold and the teachers

4. What will Maggie and Sam probably do for the next test?

    a. They will study for it together.
    b. They will try to beat one another.
    c. They will ask the teacher for help.

5. Write **T** if the statement is true and **F** if the statement is false.

    a. Sam asked Maggie to study with him first. _______
    b. Sam and Maggie got the same score. _______

Practice the Skill

Characters are the people or animals in the story. You can guess and understand the characters from what they say and do.

Fill in the blanks. Then number the sentences in order.

> best   Sam   Maggie   courage   comparing

Characters	Say	Do
__________	·( ) People won't stop ____________ us, but I don't care. ·(*1*) Let's study together.	·I found the ____________ to speak with Sam. ·I helped Sam with math and history. ·I got a better score on the test.
__________	·( ) Sure. You help me with math and history. I will help you with science. ·( ) I feel great because we did our ____________ and got better scores.	·I helped Maggie with science. ·I got a better score on the test.

Test-Wise

The following are examples of questions about characters:

Who are the two main characters?

1. Which characters are in the story?

   a. Only Maggie and Sam

   b. Maggie, Sam, and their classmates

   c. Maggie, Sam, their classmates, and Mr. Arnold

Focus on Summarizing

Complete the summary. Then rewrite it below.

Step 1

care   hated   better   decided   scores   compared

Maggie and Sam were being ____________ to one another by their classmates.

- Who were being compared?

Maggie and Sam ____________ it, so they ____________ to study together for a big test.

- What did they decide to do?

They thought that studying together can bring ____________ results. In the end, they got higher ____________, and they decided not to ____________ about being compared.

- What did they think in the end?

Step 2

Maggie and Sam were ________________________________

Both are possible answers to the question. Choose one and talk about it with your partner.

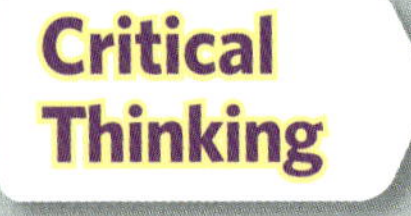

Critical Thinking

What would you say if your classmates compared you to your friends?
a. Please don't compare me to my friends.
b. I will do my best, and I don't care about it.

Don't Judge People Unfairly 

Before Reading

Predict the Text

1. Do you usually judge people by their looks?

2. Guess the story from the photo and the given words.

neighbor
- black suit
- sunglasses
- strange

Key Words to Learn

1. investigate   •   • afraid

2. mayor   •   • to study, to examine

3. terrified   •   • to be easily understood

4. make sense   •   • the chief officer of a city

5. judge   •   • not fairly, not reasonably

6. unfairly   •   • to form an opinion

Reading Skill

Characters

Characters Characters are the people or animals in the story.

Characters		A	B
Details	Looks		
	Actions		

A　Mr. Blunt was Millie's neighbor. He always came home early in the morning. He wore black sunglasses and a suit, and carried a big suitcase.

B　One morning, Millie accidentally saw Mr. Blunt with some other men. They were carrying guns! 　5　 Millie decided to **investigate** Mr. Blunt. She asked her other neighbors, but no one knew anything about him.

C　A week later, Millie was playing in her yard when Mr. Blunt came home. As he walked into 　10　 his house, he dropped **something**. Millie waited until he was inside, and then she picked it up. It was a photograph of Mr. Blunt with the **mayor**. Suddenly, Mr. Blunt was standing right behind her!

investigate

terrified

D   "Thanks," he said and took the picture.   15
Millie was **terrified**. "I'm one of the mayor's
bodyguards," he said nicely. At that moment,
everything **made sense** to Millie. She knew she
had **judged** her neighbor **unfairly**.

Words 148   **Sentences** 23

A Who are the people in the story?

What did Mr. Blunt look like?

B What did Millie decide to do?

C Who was in the picture?

D What did Millie think after she found out he was a bodyguard?

Reading Comprehension

1. What is this passage mainly about?

    a. A girl who wants to know about her neighbor
    b. A girl who meets the mayor's friend
    c. A girl who wants to be a bodyguard

2. Why does the writer describe Mr. Blunt's looks in paragraph A?

    a. To show that he looks suspicious
    b. To explain his strange schedule
    c. To show that he is in a gang

3. Millie's neighbors didn't tell her about Mr. Blunt because _______________.

    a. they are scared of him
    b. they don't know him well
    c. they have never seen him

4. What is the pronoun **something** in paragraph C referring to?

    a. a house   b. a gun   c. a photograph

5. Write **T** if the statement is true and **F** if the statement is false.

    a. Nobody knew about Mr. Blunt. _______
    b. Mr. Blunt got a picture of Millie with the mayor. _______

Practice the Skill

Characters are the people or animals in the story. You can guess and understand the characters from what they look like or what they do.

Fill in the blanks.

strange   investigated   morning   Millie   wore

Characters		_____________	Mr. Blunt
Details	Looks		He __________ sunglasses and a suit.
	Actions	She _____________ Mr. Blunt.	He came home early in the _____________.
What are they like?		curious	_____________
What words are the clues for your guess?		investigate, ask, pick up the photograph	black sunglasses, suit, gun, came home early in the morning

Test-Wise

The following are examples of questions about characters:

What is Mr. Blunt like?

What words are the clues for your guess about Mr. Blunt?

1. What is Millie like?

  a. She is curious.

  b. She is strange.

  c. She is insensitive.

Focus on Summarizing

Complete the summary. Then rewrite it below.

Step1

Millie thought her ______________, Mr. Blunt, was very strange.

- What did Millie think of Mr. Blunt?

What he did, what he ____________ like, and what he carried made her think that he was ____________.

- Why did she think that?

One day, Millie saw a photograph which he had dropped. In the picture, he was with the ____________. Mr. Blunt told her that he was a ____________. Millie felt bad about ____________ him unfairly.

- What did Millie see in Mr. Blunt's yard?

Step2

Millie thought her ____

Critical Thinking

Why is judging people only by their looks not good?
a. It is because we can misunderstand people.
b. It is because looks don't tell what people are really like.

Little Wolf and Little Red Riding Hood  Fiction

Before Reading

Predict the Text

1. Do you know the story, *Little Red Riding Hood*?

2. Guess the story from the photo and the given words.

Little Wolf

be careful

Little Red Riding Hood

Key Words to Learn

1. warn • • to see

2. chase • • to get dressed

3. spot • • in the direction of

4. toward • • to run after

5. put on • • to give trouble to

6. bother • • to say something may be dangerous

Little Wolf and Little Red Riding Hood

Fiction

T03

A One morning, Little Wolf wanted to visit his grandmother. "Watch out for Little Red Riding Hood," Little Wolf's mother **warned** him. "She **chases** little wolves and kills them!" Little Wolf promised to be careful. 5

B Little Wolf left his house. It was a lovely afternoon in the forest. The sun was shining, and birds were singing. Suddenly, Little Wolf **spotted** something red behind a tree. It was Little Red Riding Hood. She was coming **toward** him! 10

C Little Wolf ran to his grandmother's house. He told her about Little Red Riding Hood. "Hide!" **she** said and **put on** some human clothes. She looked like a real human grandmother! Suddenly, Little

bother

Fractured Fairy Tales

Fractured fairy tales are folk tales that have been changed to make people laugh. They have unexpected characterizations and plot developments, and they create different points of view. Many people now enjoy fractured fairy tales.

You can write your own fractured fairy tale.

1 Choose some famous story characters.

2 Change the roles of the characters.
e.g. Little Red Riding Hood can chase Little Wolf.

3 Change the setting of the story.

e.g. Cinderella can attend a party in Egypt.

4 Change the facts of the story.
e.g. Pinocchio can be getting taller whenever he tells lies.

5 Or combine two different fairy tales.

Create your own fractured story, and share the story with your friends.

The Farmer Who Became a Hero Fiction

Story Structure

Before Reading

Predict the Text

1. Do you like stories with happy endings?

2. Guess the story from the photo and the given words.

farmer

problem — say what he wants

hero

Key Words to Learn

1. force   • • no sound, being quiet

2. silence   • • the others that are left

3. argue   • • to make someone do something

4. stay   • • to say reasons for / against a thing

5. reward   • • to spend some time in a place

6. rest   • • getting something in return for working hard

The Farmer Who Became a Hero

Fiction · T04

Reading Skill

Story Structure: Plot

Plot The plot is the order of events. It tells what problems the characters have, and how they solve the problems.

Plot	What Happened?
Beginning	
Middle	
End	

A Rami was a farmer in ancient Egypt. Each year, he saw farmers from other villages taken away. They were **forced** to build pyramids for the king.

B One day, the king's men came to Rami's village. "All farmers must come with us," they said. "We'll build another great pyramid for our king." There was **silence**. The farmers did not want to leave, but **they** were afraid to **argue**. 5

C Rami was different. In a strong voice, he spoke up. "We farmers grow food for all of Egypt. If you take us away, soon there won't be any food left! Please, let some of us **stay**." 10

silence

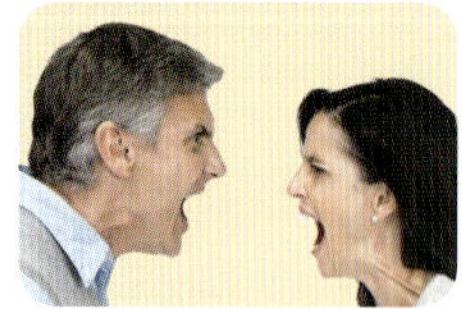

argue

D The king's men thought about this. Finally, they said, "You're right, farmer. Those who choose to help build the pyramid, come with us. You'll be **rewarded**. The **rest** of you can stay and grow food." Some farmers left, and others stayed. That night, the village celebrated. Rami became a hero!

15

Words 157   **Sentences** 21

Text Talk

A Which characters are in the story?

B Why did the king's men come to Rami's village?

C What would happen if Rami and the other farmers were forced to build pyramids?

D What happened at the end?

Reading Comprehension

1. What is this passage about?

    a. A farmer who fights a king
    b. A farmer who builds a pyramid
    c. A farmer who solves a problem

2. What is the pronoun **they** in paragraph B referring to?

    a. farmers
    b. pyramids
    c. king's men

3. What causes the problem in the story?

    a. Rami wants to be a hero.
    b. The pyramids are very difficult to build.
    c. The king's men want famers to build the pyramids.

4. The village celebrated at the end of the story because ______________.

    a. Rami became the leader of the village
    b. the farmers could stay if they wanted to
    c. all the pyramids were built

5. Write **T** if the statement is true and **F** if the statement is false.

    a. Rami already worked on a pyramid. _______
    b. Rami argued for the farmers and Egypt's food. _______

Practice the Skill

The plot is the order of events. It tells what problems the characters have, and how they solve the problems. The plot has a beginning, middle, and end.

Fill in the blanks.

> Rami's   choose   pyramids   farmers   hero   argued

Plot	
Beginning	One day, the king's men came to ___________ village. They wanted to take farmers away to build the ___________.
Middle	Rami strongly ___________ against the idea. The king's men thought about it and then let the farmers ___________ whether to leave or to stay.
End	The ___________ could decide what they wanted to do. Rami became a ___________.

Test-Wise

The following are examples of questions about plot:
What happened in the middle of the story?
What happened at the end of the story?

1. What happened at the beginning of the story?
   a. Rami became a hero.
   b. The farmers in Rami's village were all taken away.
   c. The king's men came to Rami's village.

Focus on Summarizing

Complete the summary. Then rewrite it below.

Step 1

Rami saw that ___________ were being taken away to build ___________ . Then, the king's men came to take him and other farmers in his village.

- What happened at the beginning?

However, Rami ___________ that some should ___________ and ___________ food.

- What happened in the middle of the story?

Finally, the king's men said that the farmers could choose what they would do. Rami became a ___________ .

- What happened at the end?

Step 2

Rami saw that ____

Critical Thinking

What would have happened if Rami didn't say the farmers should stay?
a. All the farmers in Rami's village would have to build the pyramids.
b. There might have been no food for the country.

32

Mr. and Mrs. Silverfox

Before Reading

Predict the Text

1. Where does your family name come from?

2. Guess the story from the photo and the given words.

Key Words to Learn

1. surname • • general, usual

2. nod • • family name

3. combine • • to join with a hyphen(-)

4. hyphenate • • to unite, to join

5. common • • by law

6. legally • • to move your head up and down to show agreement

Mr. and Mrs. Silverfox

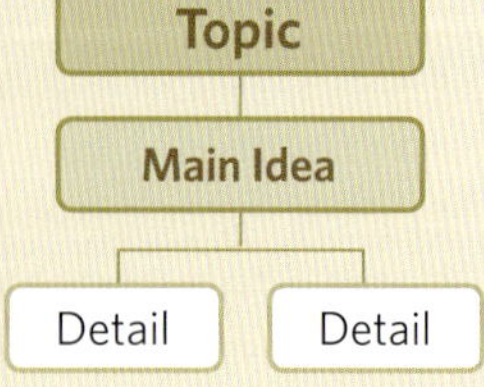

A It was the first day of 6th grade at Ocean View School in California. Sam and Emily walked home together after school.

B "I like our English teacher," said Sam, "but her name makes me laugh." Emily smiled and said, "Yeah, Mrs. Little-Baker sounds strange. If I get married, I won't change my **surname**." "Really? That's unusual in the U.S. You won't take your husband's surname?" Sam asked. Emily shook her head and replied, "No. My parents are Spanish, and most Spanish women don't change their names after marriage."

C Sam **nodded**. "In most Asian cultures women don't change their names either. But if I get married, I'll **combine** my name with my wife's." Emily replied, "So you'll have a **hyphenated** last name, like Mrs. Little-Baker? That's **common** in

Know Your Illness

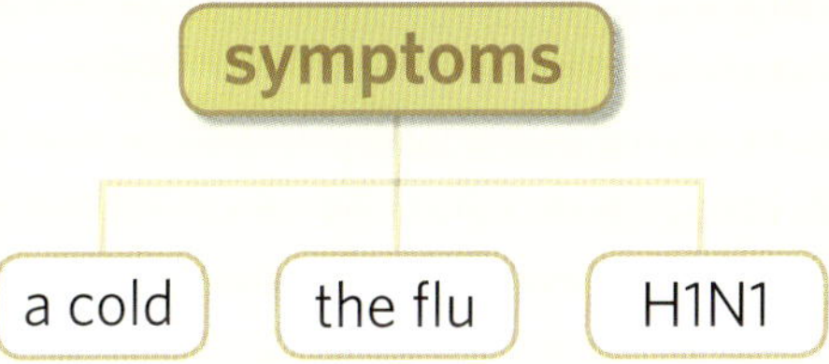

Predict the Text

1. Have you ever had a cold or the flu?

2. Guess the story from the photo and the given words.

symptoms

a cold　the flu　H1N1

Key Words to Learn

1. ache　　　　　• • to cure

2. symptom　　• • to get sick / ill

3. stuffy nose　• • a sign of disease

4. sneeze　　　• • to push a lot of air out your nose

5. diarrhea　　 • • the condition of your nose that is full and can't breathe

6. treat　　　　• • an illness that causes you to pass watery waste

Know Your Illness

Reading Skill

Main Idea & Details

Details Details are information that supports the main idea.

Main Idea
- Detail 1
- Detail 2
- Detail 3

A   You are coughing. You are tired, and your body **aches**. If you think you have a cold, you could be right or wrong. These are also **symptoms** of the flu, or even H1N1. To find out which illness you have, you have to pay careful attention to your body.

5

A Which three diseases are introduced in the paragraph?

B What are the symptoms of a cold?

C What are the symptoms of the flu?

How is the flu different from a cold?

D What are the symptoms of H1N1?

B A cold begins with a sore throat. Later, you may get a **stuffy nose**, and start coughing and **sneezing**. Your head may ache. These symptoms will **last** a few days and will go away without medicine.

C The flu arrives faster and stays longer than a cold. You will have a sore throat, a headache, or a high fever. In addition, your body will probably ache. If you feel tired and weak, you may have the flu.

D H1N1 is a serious type of flu. H1N1 can cause you to throw up or have **diarrhea**. You will likely have a high fever, a stuffy nose, a sore throat, and a cough as well. If it is not **treated** quickly, H1N1 can even lead to death.

10

15

20

Words 172   **Sentences** 17

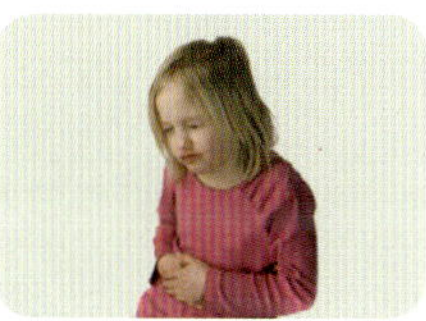
ache

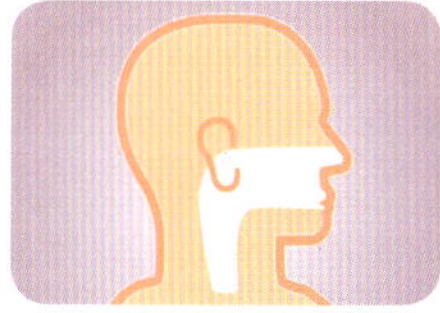
throat

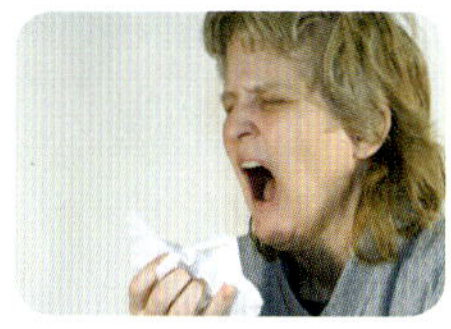
sneeze

Reading Comprehension

1. What is the purpose of this passage?

a. To discuss the dangers of H1N1
b. To explain how to treat colds and the flu
c. To show the symptoms of different diseases

2. Choose the word that can best replace **last** in paragraph B.

a. continue   b. end   c. stop

3. How is H1N1 different from a cold and the flu?

a. It doesn't cause a stuffy nose.
b. One of its symptoms is diarrhea.
c. It lasts a few days and goes away without medicine.

4. Check the correct symptoms for each illness according to the passage.

	Cold	Flu	H1N1
Stuffy Nose	✔		
Muscle Aches			
High Fever			
Diarrhea			

5. Write **T** if the statement is true and **F** if the statement is false.

a. A cold begins with a high fever. ________
b. Sometimes H1N1 leads to death. ________

Practice the Skill

Details are information that supports the main idea. Details in each paragraph help identify the main idea.

Fill in the blanks.

cold   attention   Details   flu

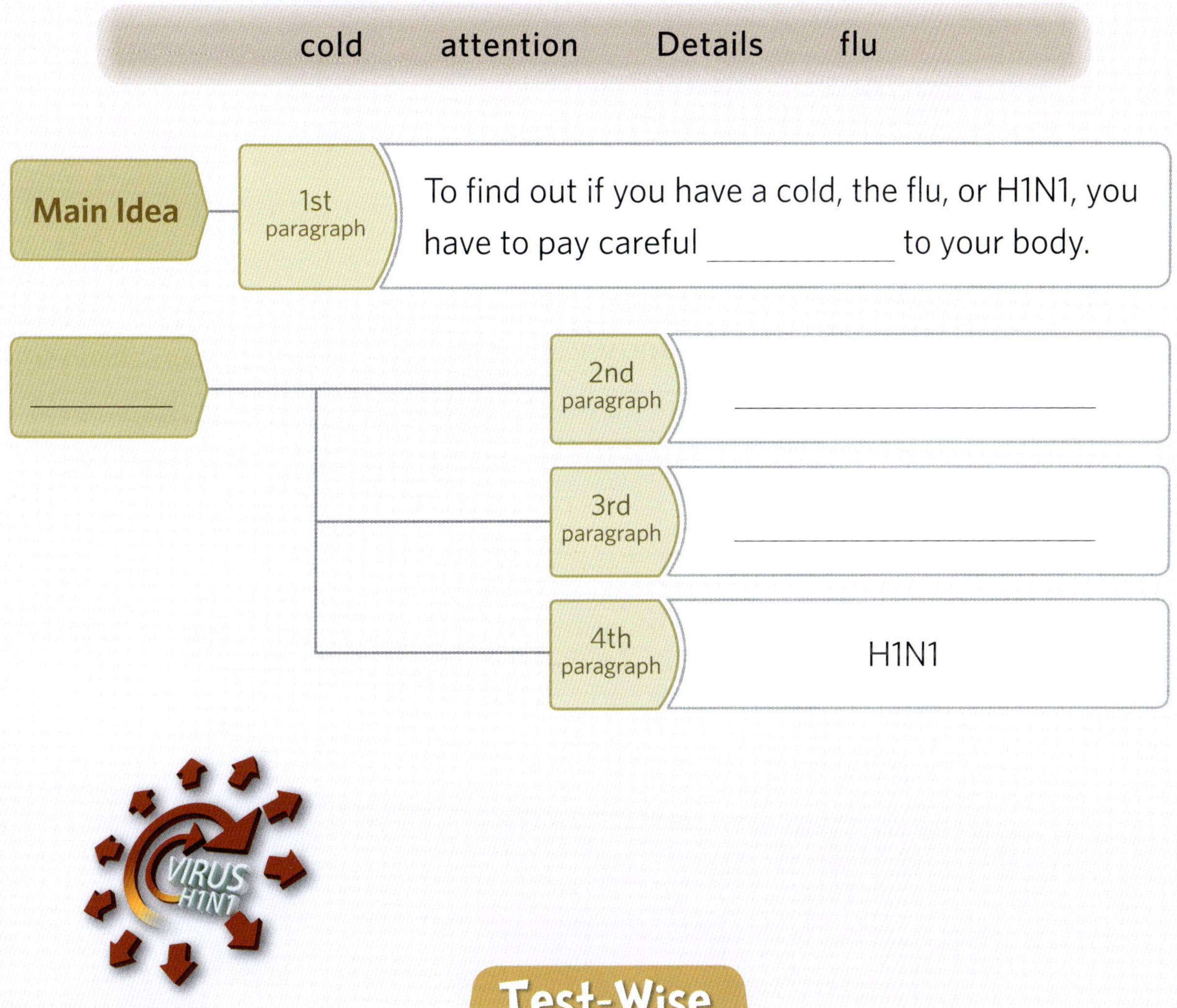

The following are examples of questions about details:

How many things does the writer discuss in the passage?

Which is the correct detail from the passage?

1. What is NOT mentioned in the passage?

a. a cold   b. the flu   c. sore eyes

Focus on Summarizing

Complete the summary. Then rewrite it below.

Step 1

The symptoms of a cold, the ____________, and H1N1 can be hard to tell apart.

- What is the main idea?

Symptoms of a cold include a ____________ throat, a ____________ nose, a cough, ____________, and a headache.

- What are the symptoms of a cold?

The flu also has ____________ like a cold, plus a high fever. Also, your body will ache.

- What are the symptoms of the flu?

Symptoms of H1N1 include throwing up, ____________, and a high fever.

- What are the symptoms of H1N1?

Step 2

The symptoms ____

Critical Thinking

Why do you think knowing the symptoms of diseases is important?
a. It is because some diseases have similar symptoms.
b. It is because some dangerous diseases have very light symptoms.

What Do Your Dreams Mean? Nonfiction

Before Reading

Predict the Text

1. Do you usually dream when you sleep?

2. Guess the story from the photo and the given words.

dream
- different cultures
- different meanings

Key Words to Learn

1. differ	being wise
2. unusual	to be different
3. illness	not common, not usual
4. loss	unhealthy condition
5. wisdom	to speak for, to mean
6. represent	a losing of things or people

What Do Your Dreams Mean? Nonfiction T07

A The way people understand dreams can **differ** from culture to culture. Some dreams, such as those about friends or family, can have the same meaning in every culture. However, what if you dream of **unusual** things?

B For example, you saw a snake in your dream. What does that mean? In Western cultures, the snake is bad luck. It means that you will experience **illness** or **loss**. In Eastern cultures, the snake means something different. In China, it is a symbol of **wisdom**. So if you dream about a snake, it means that you will become wise. In Japan, it is a sign that you will be rich.

C The elephant is another animal you might dream about. For Easterners, it **represents** something sacred. This is because Buddha was an elephant in a past life. Dreaming of an elephant shows that

Are Beavers a Frog's Best Friend?  Nonfiction

Before Reading

Predict the Text

1. Do you think beavers and frogs can be friends?

2. Guess the story from the photo and the given words.

beavers
make dams
help frogs

Key Words to Learn

1. stream	to like better
2. keep from	as something more
3. roaring	to prevent from
4. prefer	making a loud sound, crashing
5. lay eggs	to push eggs out of the body
6. in addition	a natural flow of water that is smaller than a river

Reading Skill

Main Idea & Details

Main Idea You can guess the main idea from the title and details.

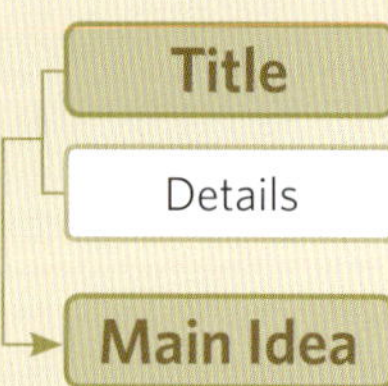

Are Beavers a Frog's Best Friend?

Nonfiction

T08

A   Life in a **stream** is difficult for frogs. The cold running water **keeps** frog babies **from** growing well. In streams, frogs also have to worry about being eaten by fish. Frogs usually sing to make friends and help 5 other frogs stay safe from fish. However, in 2007, scientists in Canada found that frogs in **roaring** streams usually do not sing much to **each other**.

B   Luckily, beavers can help! Since beavers **prefer** to live in ponds, they cut down trees with their sharp 10 teeth and create dams. Their dams turn streams into ponds and help frogs, too.

C The unmoving water of the beaver pond is much warmer than stream water. When frogs **lay** their **eggs** in the warm beaver ponds, their babies grow up healthy. **In addition**, fish do not like the pond water. Therefore, the frogs do not have to worry about being eaten.

D Clearly, life in a beaver pond is much better for frogs. Thanks to their beaver friends, frogs can sing to each other in the ponds.

Words 169   **Sentences** 14

A Why is it difficult for frogs to live in a stream?

B How do beavers make dams in streams?

C Why do frogs lay eggs in the warm beaver ponds?

D Why do you think beavers can be a frog's best friend?

stream

Reading Comprehension

1. What is the main idea of this passage?

    a. Frogs don't sing in roaring streams.
    b. Frogs prefer to live in warm ponds.
    c. Beavers build their dams, and it helps frogs, too.

2. What are the words **each other** in paragraph A referring to?

    a. scientists   b. fish   c. frogs

3. What happens after beavers build their dams?

    a. They cut down some trees.
    b. The streams become ponds.
    c. More fish enter the streams.

4. What can be inferred from the passage?

    a. Frogs can think of beavers as their friends.
    b. Beavers can think of frogs as their enemies.
    c. Frogs can think of beavers as fish.

5. Write **T** if the statement is true and **F** if the statement is false.

    a. Frogs want to lay their eggs in the warm beaver ponds. ______
    b. Life in a beaver's pond is much worse for frogs. ______

Practice the Skill

Sometimes the main idea is unstated in the story. You can guess the main idea from the title and details.

Fill in the blanks.

lay   better   help   streams   ponds   Best

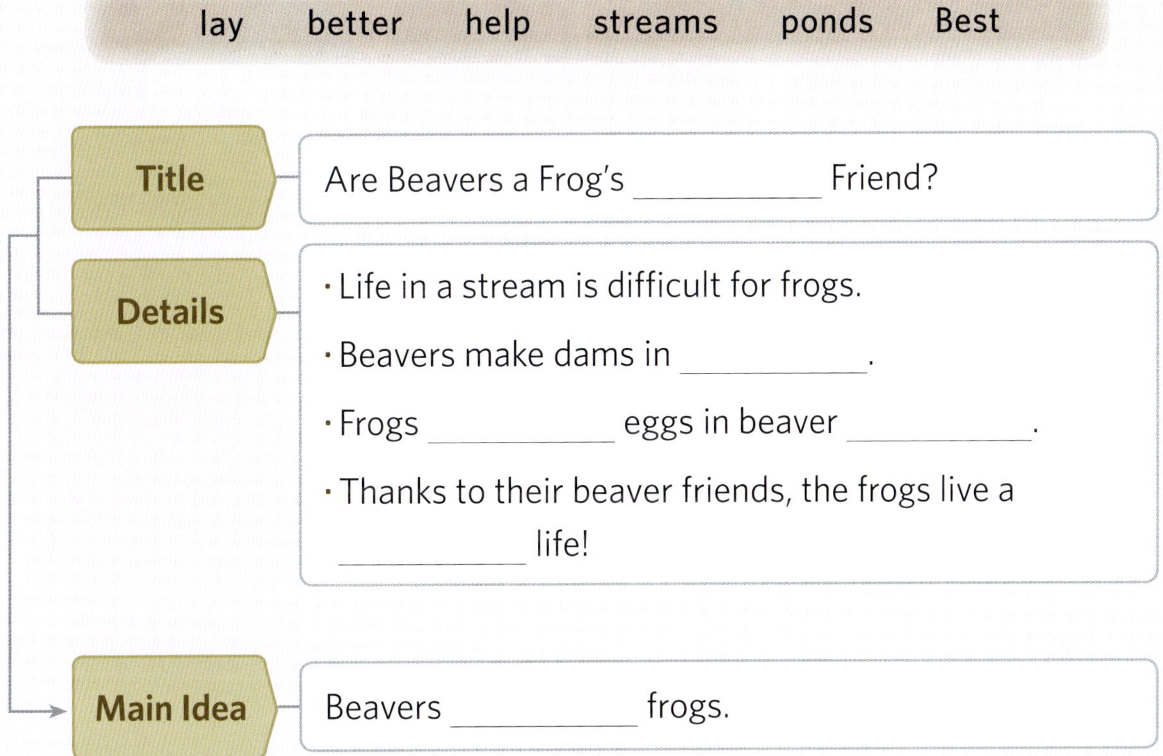

Title
Are Beavers a Frog's ___________ Friend?

Details
· Life in a stream is difficult for frogs.

· Beavers make dams in __________.

· Frogs __________ eggs in beaver __________.

· Thanks to their beaver friends, the frogs live a __________ life!

Main Idea
Beavers __________ frogs.

The following is an example of a question about the main idea:

1. What is the writer mainly talking about?
   a. Beavers' best friends
   b. Where frogs live
   c. How beavers help frogs

Focus on Summarizing

Complete the summary. Then rewrite it below.

Step1

create   dangerous   keep   fish   roaring   dams

It is ___________ for frogs to live in streams. Their babies do not grow well, and ___________ eat them. Scientists found that frogs do not sing much in ___________ streams.

- What is life like for frogs in streams?

Beavers build ___________ that are a much better place for frogs.

- How do beavers improve things for frogs?

The dams ___________ warm ponds that ___________ fish away and help frog babies grow up healthy.

- How do dams help frogs?

Step2

It is ____

Critical Thinking

Why do you think frogs should sing?
a. It is because they help each other by singing.
b. It is because they make friends by singing.

56

DINKs vs. DEWKs

Before Reading

Predict the Text

1. What do you spend money on?

2. Guess the story from the photo and the given words.

Key Words to Learn

1. shortened •   • double, two

2. advertiser •   • having a job

3. product •   • being made short

4. dual •   • a thing from a farm or factory

5. income •   • someone who tries to tell about a product

6. employed •   • money that comes from working

DINKs vs. DEWKs

Nonfiction · T09

Reading Skill

Compare & Contrast

Compare Comparing is telling how things are alike.

Contrast Contrasting is telling how things are different.

A | B

different | alike | different

A Do you know what a DINK is? What about a DEWK? These are **shortened** names that **advertisers** love to use. These names put shoppers into important categories. 5

B Companies make special **products** to attract people in these groups. DINK means "**dual income**, no kids." It is a couple in which **both** people work and make money, but they do not have 10 kids. DEWK means "dually **employed**, with kids." DEWKs work, and they have kids.

C In each type of couple, both people have a job, so they both have more money than couples with only one worker. 15 They can spend more money on products that they want.

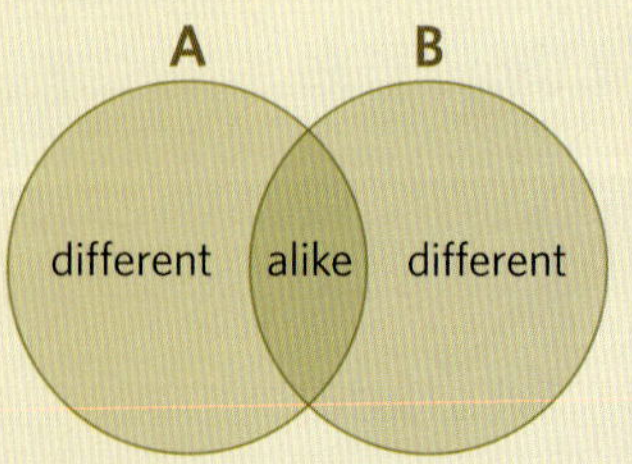

Celebrating Our Differences

Fiction

Before Reading

Predict the Text

1. Do you have any friends from different countries?

2. Guess the story from the photo and the given words.

different cultures
- differences
- similarities

Key Words to Learn

1. transfer — to move

2. arrive — to present something

3. offer — to spend time with friends

4. hang out — to get to a place

5. get used to — to think highly of someone or something

6. respect — to become familiar with

Celebrating Our Differences

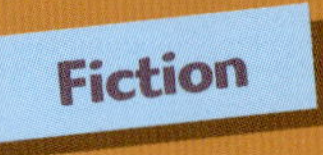

A Dear Grandfather,

B I want to tell you about Hung. He is from Vietnam, and he **transferred** to my school last month. When Hung first **arrived**, he seemed different from us. His skin was darker than ours. He made mistakes when he spoke English. 5

C At first, I did not talk much with Hung, but soon I felt bad. He had no friends to sit with at lunch or study with. I **offered** to eat with him and helped him practice English. We **hung out** every day, and soon we were best friends! 10

D Last week, I visited Hung's family. They spoke Vietnamese to each other and cooked Vietnamese noodles. They smiled when they made mistakes, while my family does not. It all felt different. However, I quickly **got used to** it! In fact, I like 15

hang out

their language, food, and culture. I like all the differences.

E　Hung's family is like our family. His family loves each other. They **respect** other people and other cultures just like us.

F　I hope you can meet Hung soon.
Love,
David

Words 173　　**Sentences** 21

Reading Comprehension

1. What is the purpose of this letter?

   a. To complain about a boy at school
   b. To describe a trip to Vietnam
   c. To tell about a new friend

2. Choose the word that can best replace **transferred** in paragraph A.

   a. moved   b. returned   c. visited

3. Why did David feel bad in paragraph C?

   a. It is because Hung spoke English very well.
   b. It is because Hung didn't make any mistakes.
   c. It is because he didn't talk much with Hung.

4. David probably thinks that we should _______________________.

   a. not make friends
   b. love differences from other cultures
   c. not tell our grandfathers about a new friend

5. Write **T** if the statement is true and **F** if the statement is false.

   a. David doesn't like other cultures. _______
   b. David is writing a letter to his grandfather about Hung and his family. _______

Practice the Skill

Comparing is telling how things are alike. Contrasting is telling how things are different. To identify what things are alike or different, we can use signal words such as *alike*, *same*, *similar*, *similarity*, *differ*, or *different*.

Fill in the blanks.

smile   Language   Vietnamese   darker   noodles   respect

	David and David's Family	Hung and Hung's Family
Skin Color	lighter	____________
____________	English	____________
Food	American food	Vietnamese ____________
Culture: make mistake	They don't ____________.	They smile.
Family	· They love each other. · They ____________ other cultures.	

Test-Wise

The following is an example of a question about compare and contrast:

1. What is the similarity between Hung's and David's family?

   a. They all respect other cultures.

   b. They eat Vietnamese noodles.

   c. They don't love each other.

Focus on Summarizing

Complete the summary. Then rewrite it below.

Step 1

| arrived | differences | friends | visited | cultures | respect |

When Hung first ___________, he seemed different from us.

- What did David think about Hung when he first arrived?

Soon after, we became best ___________. Then, I ___________ his house. His family seemed very different from my family. However, I came to like all those ___________.

- How did David's attitude change?

There are also some similarities. They ___________ other people and other ___________.

- What are the similarities between Hung's and David's family?

Step 2

When Hung first ____

Critical Thinking

Why did David like Hung's family?
a. It is because they were not very different from David's family.
b. It is because David liked all the new things about Hung's culture.

How Fast Are They?

Before Reading

Predict the Text

1. What do you think is the fastest animal in the world?

2. Guess the story from the photo and the given words.

the fastest animals

| in the air | on land | in the water |

Key Words to Learn

1. kind   •   • usually

2. normally   •   • type

3. spot   •   • to get away

4. escape   •   • a small area that has a different color

5. predator   •   • a body part which fish use to swim

6. fin   •   • an animal that eats other animals, a hunter

How Fast Are They?

Reading Skill

Compare & Contrast

Compare & Contrast
By comparing and contrasting the details, you can easily organize important information in the passage.

	A	B	C
Detail 1			
Detail 2			
Detail 3			

A What is the fastest animal on Earth? It depends on the **kind** of race: flying, running, or swimming. In the air, the peregrine falcon is the speediest. Its wings are about 40 inches long. It **normally** flies fast. However, it travels the fastest when it dives to catch other birds. During its dive, the falcon travels up to 185 miles per hour (mph). **That** is faster than a high-speed race car!

5

70

B   In a running race, the cheetah is the winner. Cheetahs have four legs and are covered with **spots**. They run fast because their favorite food, the gazelle, is fast, too. They also have to **escape** from fast **predators** like lions. Cheetahs can run at 70 mph, but only for 20 seconds. After that, they get tired.

C   Among swimmers, the sailfish holds the speed record. This fish is blue or gray and several feet long. It has a large **fin** on its back that looks like a sail. By moving its powerful tail, it can swim at 68 mph! This helps sailfish get away from predators quickly.

Words 183   **Sentences** 20

spot

peregrine falcon

fin

Reading Comprehension

1. What is the purpose of this passage?

    a. To describe how fast land animals can run
    b. To explain why birds are faster than fish
    c. To compare three of the world's fastest animals

2. What is the pronoun **That** in paragraph A referring to?

    a. 70 mph   b. 185 mph   c. 40 inches long

3. The falcon, cheetah, and sailfish are NOT compared on their ______________.

    a. color and size
    b. speed
    c. the reason why they are fast

4. Which is NOT true about the sailfish?

    a. It is the fastest sea animal.
    b. It is blue or gray.
    c. Its powerful fins don't help the sailfish to swim fast.

5. Write **T** if the statement is true and **F** if the statement is false.

    a. The peregrine falcon files fast to catch other birds. ______
    b. Cheetahs can run at 70 mph for two hours. ______

Practice the Skill

Compare & Contrast

By comparing and contrasting the details, you can easily organize important information in the passage. You can compare and contrast between two or more people, things, places, or ideas.

Circle or fill in the blanks.

68   70   185   ocean   sky   land

		Peregrine Falcon	Cheetah	Sailfish
Why are they fast?	to look for food	(Yes / No)	(Yes / No)	(Yes / No)
	to get away from predators	(Yes / No)	(Yes / No)	(Yes / No)
How fast are they?		_____ mph	_____ mph	_____ mph
Where do they live?		_______	_______	_______

Test-Wise

The following are examples of questions about compare and contrast:

What are the things that are being compared?

1. What do the peregrine falcon, cheetah, and sailfish have in common?
   a. They are the fastest in the air.
   b. They are the fastest on land.
   c. They are the fastest animals of their kind.

Focus on Summarizing

Complete the summary. Then rewrite it below.

Step 1

animals   dives   runs   land   predators   ocean   escapes

There are three categories of the fastest ___________, such as the peregrine falcon in the air, the cheetah on __________, and the sailfish in the __________.

- What are being compared?

The peregrine falcon flies the fastest when it __________ to catch other birds.

- When does the peregrine falcon fly the fastest?

The cheetah runs the fastest when it __________ after a gazelle and __________ from its predators.

- When does the cheetah run the fastest?

The sailfish swims the fastest when it tries to get away from its __________.

- When does the sailfish swim the fastest?

Step 2

There are three categories ____

Critical Thinking

Why does the writer divide the fastest animals into three categories?
a. It is because they live in different places.
b. It is because they have different physical abilities.

Cheetah

Cheetahs live in most of Africa and parts of the Middle East. Cheetahs eat hares, calves, and gazelles. Males group together with their brothers, or they join other groups of single males. Females group together with their mothers, daughters, or sisters. They also live with other female families.

hare

calf

gazelle

Peregrine Falcon

Peregrine falcons are also called duck hawks in North America. Peregrine falcons hunt small mammals like rabbits, reptiles like turtles or snakes, or insects like spiders.

Sailfish

Sailfish live in warmer areas in the oceans. They eat small fish and squids. Sailfish swim really fast and jump really high.

Nonfiction

Universal Rituals

Unit 12

Compare & Contrast

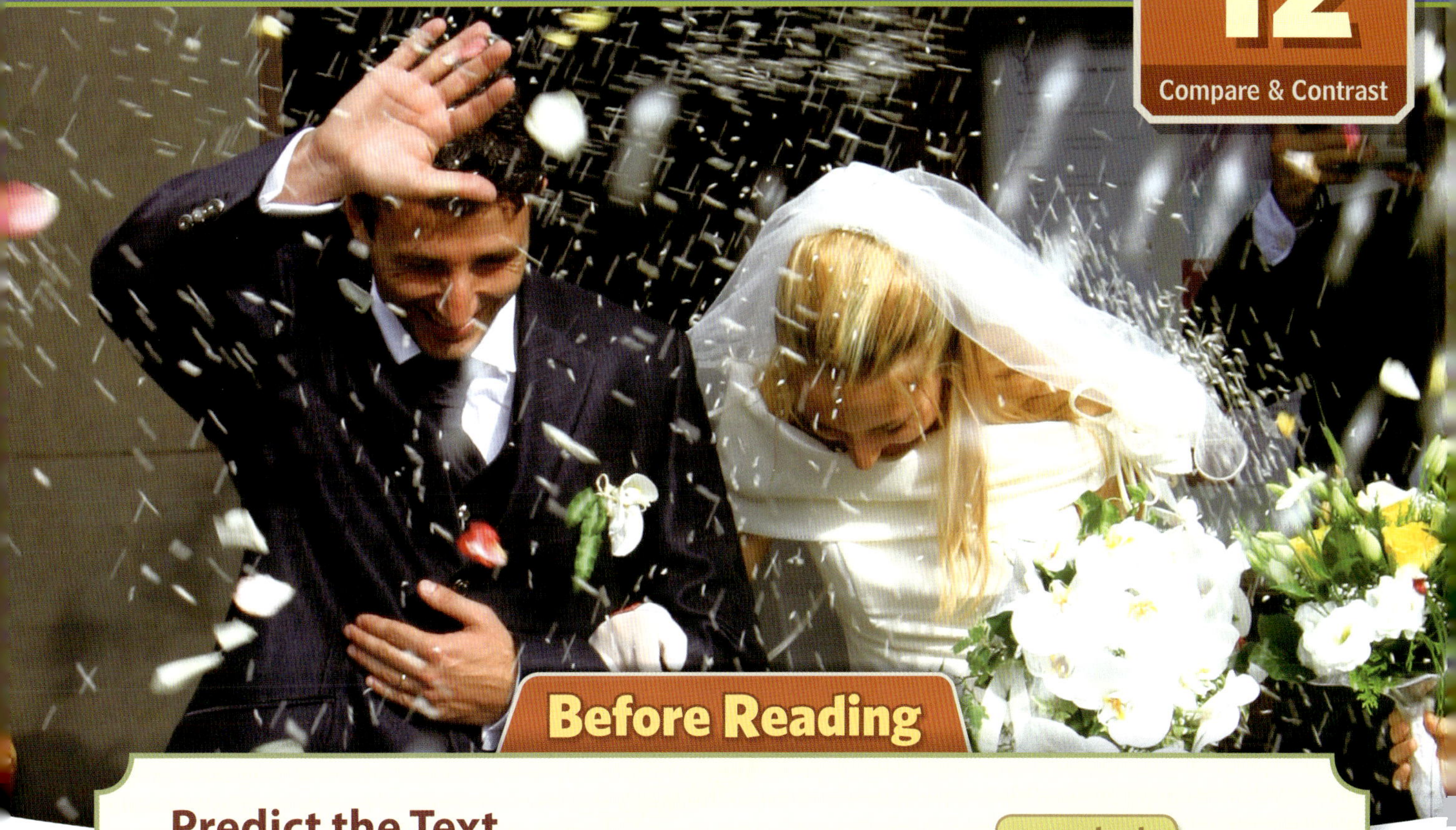

Before Reading

Predict the Text

1. Do you do something special before a big day?
2. Guess the story from the photo and the given words.

symbol

world

same | different

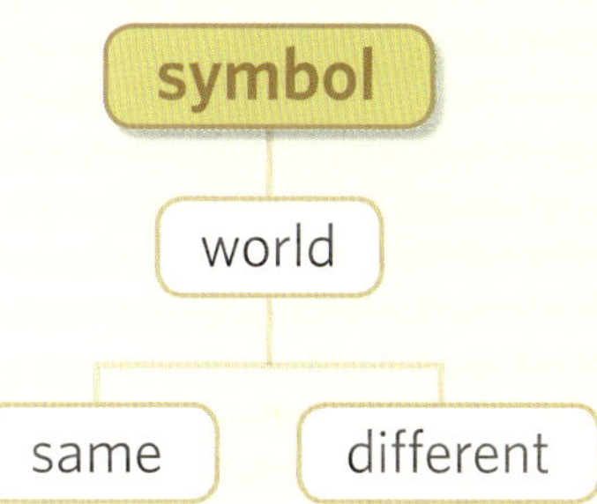

Key Words to Learn

1. realize	necessary, important
2. ritual	one part of a flower
3. symbolic	expressed by a symbol
4. petal	to understand
5. essential	a tube where blood runs through
6. vein	stereotyped behavior

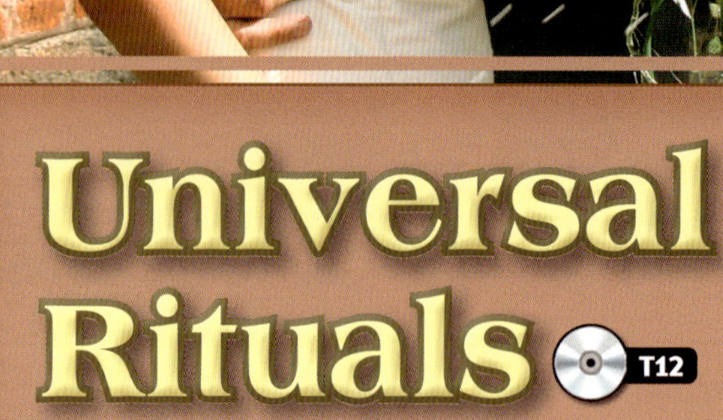

Reading Skill

Compare & Contrast

Compare & Contrast
Sometimes one big topic is the same, but the details of the topic can be different.

Same	Different
A	A-1, A-2
B	B-1, B-2

A You may not **realize** it, but the world is filled with **rituals**. Rituals are actions that have **symbolic** meanings. For example, a special dinner on Sundays can be your family ritual. However, some rituals are shared by cultures around the world.

B One example is related to wedding ceremonies. At many weddings today, you may notice that **petals** are thrown. In the East and West, people have thrown rice since ancient times. Rice grows

78

What to Do in an Earthquake  Fiction

Before Reading

Predict the Text

1. Have you ever heard about any earthquakes recently?

2. Guess the story from the photo and the given words.

- earthquake
  - what to do
    - blanket
    - run to a corner
    - run to higher ground

Key Words to Learn

1. plate   •   • if

2. shelf   •   • to come after

3. blanket   •   • to keep from danger

4. protect   •   • an item used to put food on

5. follow   •   • a soft and warm piece of fabric

6. in case   •   • a flat surface used for keeping small things

What to Do in an Earthquake

Fiction

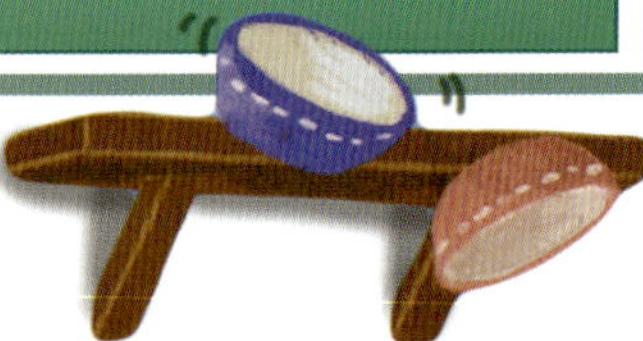

Reading Skill

Sequence

Sequence The sequence is the order of events in the story.

Time Signal Words first, next, after that, finally

First
↓
Next
↓
After that
↓
Finally

A One morning, my family was eating breakfast. We were talking and laughing as normal. Suddenly, everything started shaking. **Plates** and books fell off the **shelves**. It was an earthquake! I was very scared. 5

B "Quickly, children," my father said, "Do as I say, and we'll all be safe." First, we ran to a corner far inside the house. This was a safe place. It was away from windows and furniture that could fall on us. Next, we used **blankets** to **protect** our heads 10 and necks. The ground stopped shaking after a while.

C After that, we **followed** my father outside. "It's not safe to stay in the house," he said, "It could fall down." Once we were outside, we had to worry 15

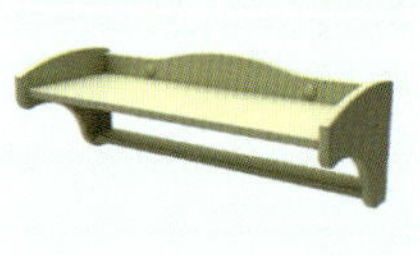

shelf

tsunami

about a tsunami. This was because my house is near the ocean.

D   Finally, we ran together to higher ground. We were safe **there** **in case** the ocean waters started to rise.

20

Words 155   **Sentences** 18

A What happened to the writer's family?

B What did the family do first?

What did the family do next?

C What did the family have to worry about?

D What was the final thing the family did?

Reading Comprehension

1. What is this passage mainly about?

    a. How earthquakes can cause tsunamis
    b. How a family stayed safe during an earthquake
    c. How a child's city was destroyed by an earthquake

2. How did the writer feel after the earthquake started?

    a. cheerful   b. bored   c. frightened

3. What did the family do when the earthquake stopped?

    a. They left the house.
    b. They picked up the books and plates.
    c. They ran to a corner far inside the house.

4. What is the word **there** in paragraph D referring to?

    a. the house   b. the ocean   c. higher ground

5. Write **T** if the statement is true and **F** if the statement is false.

    a. Earthquakes can cause windows to break. _______
    b. A tsunami destroyed the writer's house. _______

Practice the Skill

The sequence is the order of events in the story. To identify the order, we can use time signal words such as *first*, *next*, *after that*, or *finally*.

Fill in the blanks. Then number the events in order.

First   escape   Next   Finally   Earthquake   protect

What to Do in an ________________

________________, run to a safe corner far inside the house.

________________, run to higher ground in case there is a tsunami.

________________, use blankets to ________________ our heads and necks.

After that, go outside to ________________ in case the house falls down.

Test-Wise

The following are examples of questions about sequence:

What did they do after they ran to a corner?

1. What was the first thing the writer's family did when the earthquake happened?

   a. They all went outside.

   b. They went to higher ground.

   c. They went to a corner far inside the house.

Focus on Summarizing

Complete the summary. Then rewrite it below.

Step 1

protected   safe   earthquake   Next   finally

When the earthquake happened, my family first went to a ___________ place in my house.

• What did the family do first?

___________, we ___________ our heads and necks.

• What did the family do next?

After that, when the ___________ stopped, we got out of the house.

• What did the family do when the earthquake stopped?

We worried about a tsunami, so ___________ we moved to higher ground.

• Finally, what did the family do?

Step 2

When the earthquake ___________________________

Why do you think it is important to follow simple steps in an emergency?
a. It is because we should protect ourselves.
b. It is because it helps people think clearly about what to do.

Finding Courage by Working Together

Fiction

Unit 14

Sequence

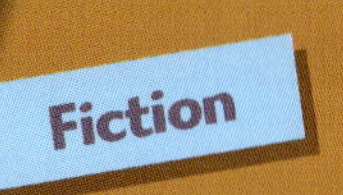

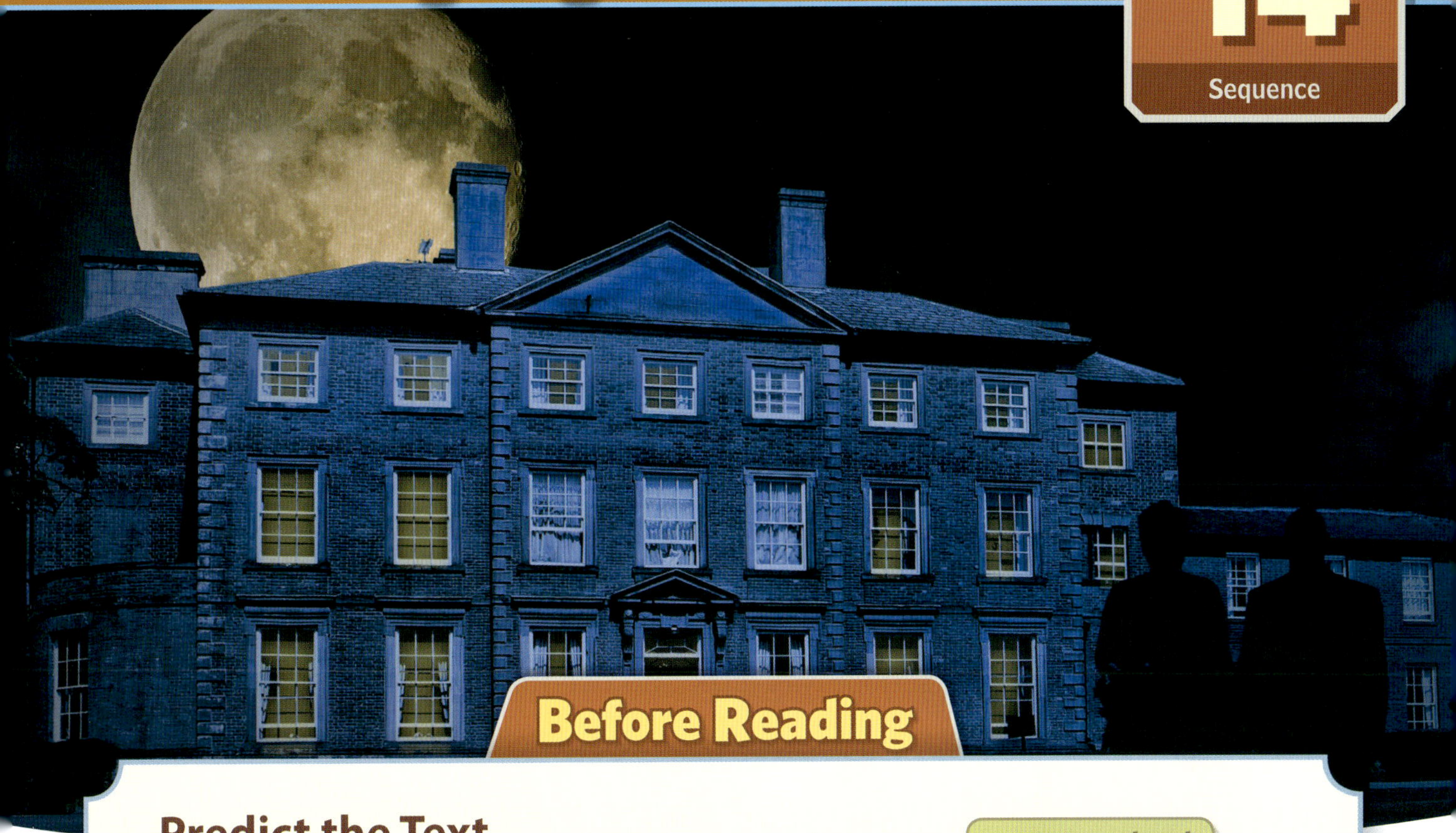

Before Reading

Predict the Text

1. Are you afraid of ghosts?

2. Guess the story from the photo and the given words.

courage test

find the gold coins

Key Words to Learn

1. cemetery	to finish
2. frightened	to get to
3. beneath	believed to be visited by ghosts
4. reach	afraid, terrified, scared
5. haunted	a place where dead people are buried
6. complete	below, under

Finding Courage by Working Together `Fiction` T14

A During summer vacation, the 6th-grade students went to school. They took a courage test. Their teachers told them to find three gold coins. The school was dark and decorated to look scary. The students had to work together to find the coins. 5

B First, the students went to the cafeteria. It looked like a **cemetery**! They were **frightened**. They felt like dead people would rise from their tombs. One of the students found the first gold coin behind a tombstone. 10

C After that, they entered the music room. It looked like a ghost forest! Again, the students were terrified. In spite of their fear, they found the second gold coin. It was shining **beneath** a tree.

D Finally, they **reached** the gym. There were scary 15 noises coming from a stereo. It looked like a

frightened

cemetery

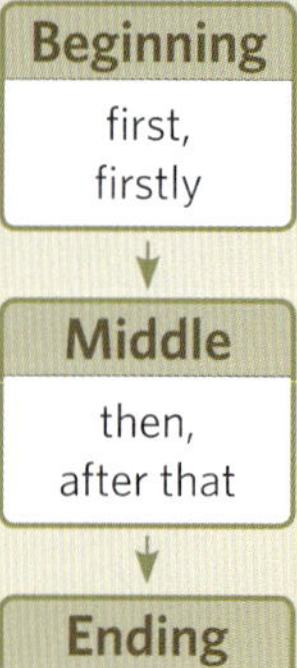

Fast Changes in the World of Cell Phones

Predict the Text

1. How often do you use a cell phone?

2. Guess the story from the photo and the given words.

cell phone

- first cell phone
- flip phone
- smart-phone

Key Words to Learn

1. weigh	to continue in time
2. last	an act of turning over
3. despite	to shake continuously
4. flip	in spite of
5. text	to have a specific weight
6. vibrate	a text message

Reading Skill

Sequence

Sequence The sequence is the order of events in the story.

Time Signal Words To identify the order, we can use time signal words.

Months	Years
January, February	In 1983, In 1996

A You are walking home from school. Suddenly, you notice a strange person following you! What would you do? With your cell phone, you can call for help. However, thirty years ago, <u>this</u> was not possible. Since then, cell phones have 5 become important in our lives.

B In 1983, the first cell phone went on sale. It was ten inches long and **weighed** over two pounds. Its battery **lasted** only one hour. It cost $4,000! **Despite** the high price, many people bought one. 10

Make Your Own Delicious Dessert! 

Predict the Text

1. Do you like desserts?

2. Guess the story from the photo and the given words.

shortbread squares
- shortbread
- caramel
- chocolate

Key Words to Learn

1. treat	to become watery
2. layer	made beforehand
3. pre-made	something that covers a surface
4. pour	to make something flow
5. melt	to make bright (**opp.** darken)
6. brighten	a special and delicious food or drink

Make Your Own Delicious Dessert! T16

Nonfiction

Reading Skill

Sequence

Sequence The sequence is the order of events in the story.

Time Signal Words
Some time signal words such as *while* or *during* describe that the events are happening at the same time.

A ⟶ while B
⟶ next

A Do you know what a caramel shortbread square is? It is a **treat** with three **layers**: shortbread, caramel, and chocolate. It is crunchy and sweet. It tastes nutty, chocolatey, and delicious. Best of all, you can easily make it at home! 5

B

Here is what you will need:

- a pan
- a pot
- half a cup of butter
- half a cup of brown sugar 10
- 2 tablespoons of syrup
- 1 cup of milk
- 2 big bars of chocolate
- **pre-made** shortbread
- almonds or walnuts 15

102

C   Here is what you do.
First, make the caramel.
Mix the butter, sugar,
syrup, and milk in a pot.
Then, heat **it** for about ten   20
minutes. While heating the caramel, put the
pre-made shortbread in the bottom of the pan.
After the caramel is made, **pour** it onto the
shortbread. Finally, heat the chocolate bars
until they are **melted**. Pour them on top of the   25
caramel. If you want, you can put almonds or
walnuts on top. When everything has cooled for
a while, cut your shortbread into small squares.
This tasty treat is sure to **brighten** your day!

Words 181   **Sentences** 16

Text Talk

A What is this passage about?

B What do you need to make shortbread squares?

C What words help you understand the order of the cooking steps?

pour

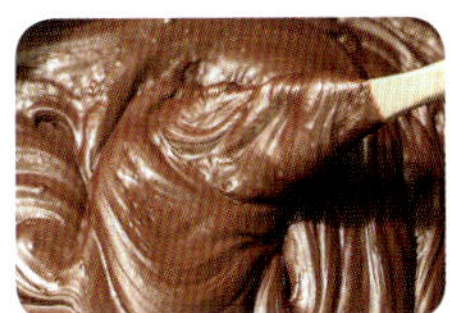

melt

Reading Comprehension

1. What is the purpose of this passage?

   a. To teach someone how to bake
   b. To describe a dessert
   c. To explain how to make shortbread squares

2. What should be done first?

   a. Make the caramel.
   b. Place some shortbread in a pan.
   c. Melt the chocolate.

3. What is the pronoun **it** in paragraph C referring to?

   a. milk   b. caramel   c. butter

4. Why should you wait before cutting the squares?

   a. It is because they are too cold.
   b. It is because they taste better before cutting.
   c. It is because they need to cool off first.

5. Write **T** if the statement is true and **F** if the statement is false.

   a. Nuts can be added with the chocolate. _______
   b. Caramel shortbread squares have two layers. _______

Practice the Skill

The sequence is the order of events in the story. To identify the order, we can use time signal words. Some time signal words such as *while* or *during* describe that the events are happening at the same time.

Number the events in order.

First, make the caramel.

Put the pre-made shortbread in the pan.

Then, heat the caramel for 10 minutes.

When everything has cooled, cut it into small squares.

Finally, melt the chocolate and pour it onto the caramel.

After the caramel is made, pour it onto the shortbread.

Test-Wise

The following are examples of questions about sequence:

Which two things do you have to do at the same time when you make shortbread squares?

1. Number the steps in the correct order.

a. While heating the caramel, put the pre-made shortbread in the pan. ______

b. Heat the caramel for about 10 minutes. ______

c. After the caramel is made, pour it onto the shortbread. ______

Focus on Summarizing

Complete the summary. Then rewrite it below.

Step 1

| put | While | First | Finally | pour | steps | melt |

There are three main __________ to making caramel shortbread squares. __________, make the caramel. Then heat it for a while.

- What do you have to do first?

__________ heating the caramel, __________ the pre-made shortbread in the pan. After the caramel is made, pour it onto the shortbread.

- What do you have to do next?

__________, __________ some chocolate and __________ that onto the caramel. When everything has cooled for a while, cut your shortbread into small squares.

- Finally, what do you have to do?

Step 2

There are three main ____

Why is it important to follow steps when making something?
a. By following the steps, we will not miss any important steps.
b. It is always easy to follow steps.

Get Your Head Out of the Clouds  Nonfiction

Predict the Text

1. Do you often imagine something to make yourself feel happy?

2. Guess the story from the photo and the given words.

imagine
- make you happy
- make you unhappy

Key Words to Learn

1. daydream	the time gone by
2. past	to make understandable
3. less	a specialist of psychology
4. psychologist	not so much
5. explain	a very short period of time
6. moment	to imagine happy things while awake

Get Your Head Out of the Clouds

A **Daydreaming** is fun. It lets you imagine amazing things. It also helps you remember fun things from the **past**. However, a new study about daydreaming says that it can make you **less** happy.

Improve Your Memory with Regular Exercise

Predict the Text

1. Do you like exercising?

2. Guess the story from the photo and the given words.

exercise

blood to the brain

better memory

Key Words to Learn

1. injured	a cell in the brain
2. neuron	hurt
3. store	to make structured
4. organize	to take in
5. theory	a thing
6. material	a proposed explanation

Improve Your Memory with Regular Exercise

Reading Skill

Cause & Effect

Cause & Effect
A cause is why something happens. An effect is the result.

Signal Words
because, since, if, in order to, as a result

Cause		Effect
since, if, because	→	as a result, so

A   We all know that exercising helps us stay healthy. It keeps us from getting sick or **injured**. Did you know that exercise can help your memory, too?

B   There are many reasons for this. First, exercise moves more blood to your brain. The blood carries oxygen, and **this** helps your brain work better. Also, there are tiny cells in the brain called **neurons**. Neurons **store** and **organize** memories. A **theory** suggests that exercise helps create more neurons. With more neurons, you can remember things better.

Do you want to have a photographic memory?

When you read books or think about what you did today, that information is briefly stored in your short-term memory. However, you will forget these memories soon. How can you remember things after months, or years have passed? That requires your long-term memory.

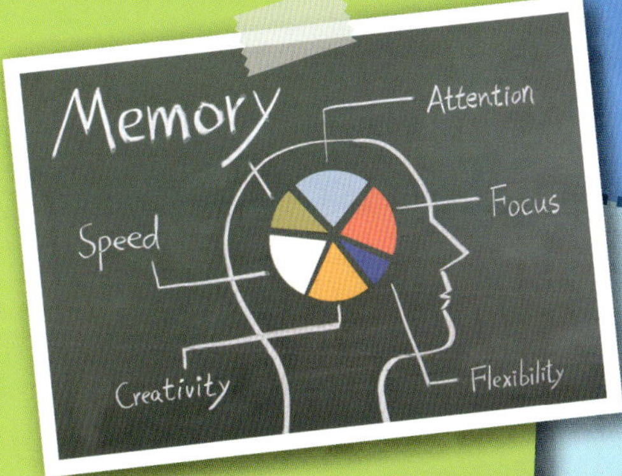

To store something in your long-term memory:

1. You have to read it over and over again.

2. You have to remember it as a special episode or as a part of your life history.

Memory

Short-Term Memory

- what you did
- what you read
- the phone numbers of the stores on the street

Long-Term Memory

Episode

- big events that you can't forget

Knowledge

- your phone number
- things you studied over and over again
- where you live

Are Scientists Evil Geniuses?

Nonfiction

Unit 19

Cause & Effect

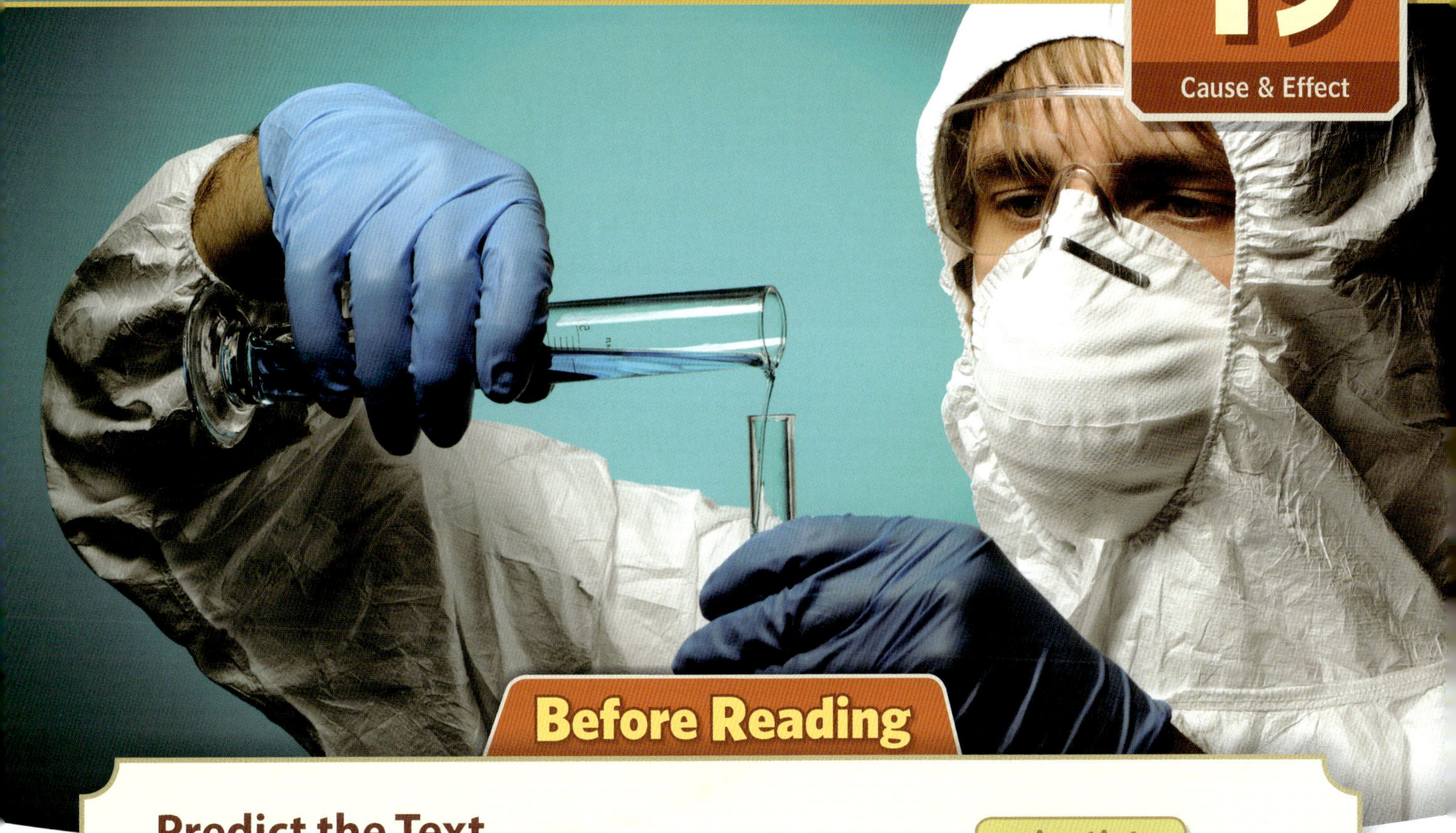

Before Reading

Predict the Text

1. Do you think scientists only make good things?

2. Guess the story from the photo and the given words.

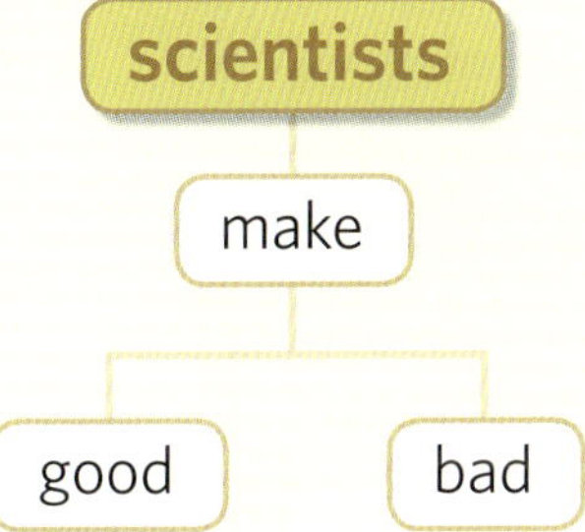

Key Words to Learn

1. invent	giving help
2. helpful	to create, to produce
3. nuclear	to find mistake with
4. destroy	powered by atomic energy
5. accident	to badly damage something
6. blame	an event that happens unexpectedly

Are Scientists Evil Geniuses? T19

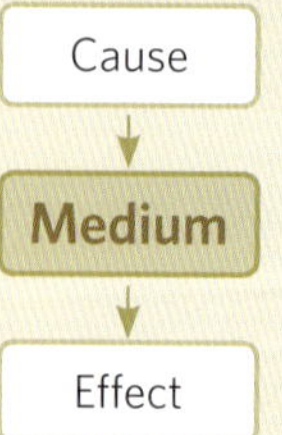

A Scientists have **invented** a number of **helpful** things for people. They have positively changed our lives. Electricity, cars, and medicine are just a few examples. However, **they** have also made some very dangerous things. Does this mean that scientists are evil geniuses? 5

B Think about Albert Einstein. He was a brilliant scientist. In the 1940s, he helped America build the first **nuclear** bomb because he did not want Germany to have the first bomb. In 1945, America dropped two nuclear bombs on Japan. The bombs ended World War II, but they also killed thousands of people. Today, there are many nuclear bombs in the world. Everyone worries that they will **destroy** the Earth one day. 10 15

How a Golden Apple Started a War  Nonfiction

Before Reading

Predict the Text

1. Do you know about the Trojan War?

2. Guess the story from the photo and the given words.

a golden apple

the most beautiful

Trojan War

Key Words to Learn

1. ancient • • difficulty

2. except for • • a female god

3. trouble • • besides, but for

4. goddess • • dating from a time long past

5. in return • • to begin fighting against a person or thing

6. attack • • in exchange for doing something

How a Golden Apple Started a War

Reading Skill

Cause & Effect

Cause & Effect
A story has a series of events that affect each other. Sometimes an effect becomes the cause of another event.

Cause	Effect

A   According to a myth, an apple once started a war. It all started at a wedding in **ancient** Greece. All the gods were invited, **except for** <u>one</u>. No one invited Eris because she liked to cause **trouble**.

B   Eris was mad about this. So, she sent a golden apple to the wedding. A note on the apple said, "For the most beautiful."

C   Three powerful **goddesses**, Hera, Athena, and Aphrodite, all wanted the apple. Each thought she was the most beautiful. They asked Zeus, the king of the gods, to judge their beauty. However, he chose Paris to be the judge. Paris was the son of the king of Troy.

ancient

attack

D   Hera, Athena, and Aphrodite visited Paris. Each goddess promised him something **in return** for the golden apple. In the end, Paris chose Aphrodite. She promised him Helen, the world's most beautiful woman.   20

E   Helen was already married to someone else, but the gods brought her to Troy. Helen's husband was very mad. He took an army and **attacked** Troy. This started one of the biggest wars in ancient history, the Trojan War.   25

Words 180   **Sentences** 20

A   Who wasn't invited to the wedding?

B   What did Eris send to the wedding?

C   Who was chosen to be the judge by Zeus?

D   What did Aphrodite promise Paris?

E   Who started the Trojan War and why?

Reading Comprehension

1. What is the topic of this passage?

    a. The different gods of ancient Greece
    b. Causes of the Trojan War
    c. Religion in the city of Troy

2. What is the pronoun **one** in paragraph A referring to?

    a. Eris   b. war   c. Greece

3. Why did Eris send a golden apple to the wedding?

    a. She wanted to give a present to the gods.
    b. She wanted to make the goddesses fight.
    c. She wanted to prove she was the most beautiful.

4. What happened after Helen was taken to Troy?

    a. Paris thanked the gods.
    b. A beauty contest was held.
    c. Helen's husband took an army and attacked Troy.

5. Write **T** if the statement is true and **F** if the statement is false.

    a. Zeus judged the goddesses' beauty. _______
    b. Aphrodite won the golden apple. _______

Practice the Skill

A story has a series of events that affect each other. Sometimes an effect becomes the cause of another event.

Fill in the blanks. Then match each cause with its effect.

invited   apple   wedding   cause   return   began

Cause

Effect

Eris liked to ___________ trouble.

The Trojan War ___________.

Eris was mad for not being ___________.

She promised him Helen in ___________.

Paris chose Aphrodite as the most beautiful.

She sent a golden ___________.

Helen's husband got mad about losing Helen.

She wasn't invited to an important ___________.

Test-Wise

The following is an example of a question about cause and effect:

1. What caused Paris to begin the Trojan War?

   a. He wanted to get the golden apple.

   b. He took another man's wife.

   c. He wanted to be the most powerful man.

Focus on Summarizing

Complete the summary. Then rewrite it below.

Step 1

fight　　invited　　Helen　　attack　　Aphrodite　　husband

The Greek goddess Eris was not ___________ to a wedding, so she was mad about this.

• What first caused these events to happen?

She made Hera, Athena, and Aphrodite ___________ over who was the most beautiful.

• Why did the three goddesses fight?

Paris, the son of Troy King, picked ___________ as the most beautiful. In return, Aphrodite sent ___________ to Paris.

• Who was the judge?

However, Helen was already married. Her ___________ got angry and took an army to ___________ Troy.

• Who was the judge?

Step 2

The Greek goddess ____

Critical Thinking

What caused the Trojan War?
a. Not inviting Eris to the wedding
b. Promising Helen to Paris

132

Word		Definition	Translation
Unit 1			
compare	*verb*	to say how things are the same or different	
curious	*adjective*	eager to know	
courage	*noun*	having no fear, bravery	
announce	*verb*	to make known publicly	
result	*noun*	the final score on something	
tie	*noun*	the same score	
Unit 2			
investigate	*verb*	to study, to examine	
mayor	*noun*	the chief officer of a city	
terrified	*adjective*	afraid	
make sense	*verb*	to be easily understood	
judge	*verb*	to form an opinion	
unfairly	*adverb*	not fairly, not reasonably	
Unit 3			
warn	*verb*	to say something may be dangerous	
chase	*verb*	to run after	
spot	*verb*	to see	
toward	*preposition*	in the direction of	
put on	*verb*	to get dressed	
bother	*verb*	to give trouble to	
Unit 4			
force	*verb*	to make someone do something	
silence	*noun*	no sound, being quiet	
argue	*verb*	to say reasons for / against a thing	
stay	*verb*	to spend some time in a place	
reward	*noun*	getting something in return for working hard	
rest	*noun*	the others that are left	
Unit 5			
surname	*noun*	family name	
nod	*verb*	to move your head up and down to show agreement	
combine	*verb*	to unite, to join	
hyphenate	*verb*	to join with a hyphen(-)	
common	*adjective*	general, usual	
legally	*adverb*	by law	

Word		Definition	Translation
Unit 6			
ache	*verb*	to get sick / ill	
symptom	*noun*	a sign of disease	
stuffy nose	*noun*	the condition of your nose that is full and can't breathe	
sneeze	*verb*	to push a lot of air out your nose	
diarrhea	*noun*	an illness that causes you to pass watery waste	
treat	*verb*	to cure	
Unit 7			
differ	*verb*	to be different	
unusual	*adjective*	not common, not usual	
illness	*noun*	unhealthy condition	
loss	*noun*	a losing of things or people	
wisdom	*noun*	being wise	
represent	*verb*	to speak for, to mean	
Unit 8			
stream	*noun*	a natural flow of water that is smaller than a river	
keep from	*verb*	to prevent from	
roaring	*adjective*	making a loud sound, crashing	
prefer	*verb*	to like better	
lay eggs	*verb*	to push eggs out of the body	
in addition	*adverb*	as something more	
Unit 9			
shortened	*adjective*	being made short	
advertiser	*noun*	someone who tries to tell about a product	
product	*noun*	a thing from a farm or factory	
dual	*adjective*	double, two	
income	*noun*	money that comes from working	
employed	*adjective*	having a job	
Unit 10			
transfer	*verb*	to move	
arrive	*verb*	to get to a place	
offer	*verb*	to present something	
hang out	*verb*	to spend time with friends	
get used to	*verb*	to become familiar with	
respect	*verb*	to think highly of someone or something	

Word		Definition	Translation
Unit 11			
kind	*noun*	type	
normally	*adverb*	usually	
spot	*noun*	a small area that has a different color	
escape	*verb*	to get away	
predator	*noun*	an animal that eats other animals, a hunter	
fin	*noun*	a body part which fish use to swim	
Unit 12			
realize	*verb*	to understand	
ritual	*noun*	stereotyped behavior	
symbolic	*adjective*	expressed by a symbol	
petal	*noun*	one part of a flower	
essential	*adjective*	necessary, important	
vein	*noun*	a tube where blood runs through	
Unit 13			
plate	*noun*	an item used to put food on	
shelf	*noun*	a flat surface used for keeping small things	
blanket	*noun*	a soft and warm piece of fabric	
protect	*verb*	to keep from danger	
follow	*verb*	to come after	
in case	*adverb*	if	
Unit 14			
cemetery	*noun*	a place where dead people are buried	
frightened	*adjective*	afraid, terrified, scared	
beneath	*preposition*	below, under	
reach	*verb*	to get to	
haunted	*adjective*	believed to be visited by ghosts	
complete	*verb*	to finish	
Unit 15			
weigh	*verb*	to have a specific weight	
last	*verb*	to continue in time	
despite	*preposition*	in spite of	
flip	*noun*	an act of turning over	
text	*noun*	a text message	
vibrate	*verb*	to shake continuously	

Word		Definition	Translation
Unit 16			
treat	*noun*	a special and delicious food or drink	
layer	*noun*	something that covers a surface	
pre-made	*adjective*	made beforehand	
pour	*verb*	to make something flow	
melt	*verb*	to become watery	
brighten	*verb*	to make bright (opp. darken)	
Unit 17			
daydream	*verb*	to imagine happy things while awake	
past	*noun*	the time gone by	
less	*adverb*	not so much	
psychologist	*noun*	a specialist of psychology	
explain	*verb*	to make understandable	
moment	*noun*	a very short period of time	
Unit 18			
injured	*adjective*	hurt	
neuron	*noun*	a cell in the brain	
store	*verb*	to take in	
organize	*verb*	to make structured	
theory	*noun*	a proposed explanation	
material	*noun*	a thing	
Unit 19			
invent	*verb*	to create, to produce	
helpful	*adjective*	giving help	
nuclear	*adjective*	powered by atomic energy	
destory	*verb*	to badly damage something	
accident	*noun*	an event that happens unexpectedly	
blame	*verb*	to find mistake with	
Unit 20			
ancient	*adjective*	dating from a time long past	
except for	*preposition*	besides, but for	
trouble	*noun*	difficulty	
goddess	*noun*	a female god	
in return	*adverb*	in exchange for doing something	
attack	*verb*	to begin fighting against a person or thing	

LEVEL GUIDE NE_Build & Grow Products

The colored level bands are transcribed as ● marks in the level columns.

| Category | Level | | Kindergarten | Primary | | | | | | Secondary | | Components |
	Books	Lexile®		Low Beginner	Beginner	High Beginner	Low Intermediate	Intermediate	High Intermediate	A	B	
Phonics	Phonics Show 1,2,3,4		●	●								Student Book/ Workbook/ 2 MultiROMs
Phonics	Phonics Show Readers 1,2,3,4		●	●								Book/ Audio CD
Phonics	Come On, Phonics 1, 2, 3, 4, 5		●	●								Student Book/ Workbook/ Readers/ DVD-ROM
Readers	Show Time L1,2,3		●	●	●	●						Student Book/ Workbook/ MultiROM
Coursebook	Come On, Everyone 1,2			●								Student Book/ Workbook/ Teacher's Book / DVD-ROM
Coursebook	Come On, Everyone 3,4				●							Student Book/ Workbook/ Teacher's Book / DVD-ROM
Coursebook	Come On, Everyone 5,6					●						Student Book/ Workbook/ Teacher's Book / DVD-ROM
Reading	Reading Sketch Starter 1,2,3	BR	●	●								Student Book/ Workbook/ MultiROM
Reading	Reading Sketch 1,2,3	170L~210L		●	●							Student Book/ Workbook/ Audio CD
Reading	Reading Sketch Up 1,2,3	260L~300L			●	●						Student Book/ Workbook/ Audio CD
Reading	Reading Sponge 1,2,3	160L~280L		●	●							Student Book/ Workbook/ MultiROM
Reading	Read & Retell 1,2,3	240L~390L			●	●						Student Book/ Workbook/ Audio CD
Reading	Reading Sense 1,2,3	320L~410L			●	●						Student Book/ Workbook/ Audio CD
Reading	Reading Clue 1,2,3	490L~510L				●	●					Student Book/ Workbook/ Audio CD
Reading	The Basic Way 1,2,3 (2nd Edition)	570L~660L				●	●					Student Book/ Workbook/ MultiROM
Reading	Read to Reach 1,2,3	600L~660L					●					Student Book/ Workbook/ Audio CD
Reading	The Best Way 1,2,3 (2nd Edition)	860L~970L							●	●		Student Book/ Workbook/ MultiROM
Reading	Reading Source 1,2,3	580L~710L					●	●				Student Book/ Workbook/ Audio CD
Reading	Reading Peak 1,2,3	860L~900L							●	●		Student Book/ Workbook/ Audio CD
Reading											●	Student Book/ Supplementary…

Category	Series	Lexile	Components
	Easy Link Starter 1,2,3		MultiROM
	Easy Link 1,2,3	240L~280L	Student Book/ Workbook/ MultiROM
	Easy Link 4,5,6	320L~380L	Student Book/ Workbook/ MultiROM
	Subject Link Starter 1,2,3	430L~460L	Student Book/ Workbook/ MultiROM
	Subject Link 1,2,3	520L~610L	Student Book/ Workbook/ Audio CD
	Subject Link 4,5,6	720L~830L	Student Book/ Workbook/ Audio CD
	Subject Link 7,8,9	860L~950L	Student Book/ Workbook/ Audio CD
Listening	Listening Seed 1,2,3		Student Book/ Workbook/ Scripts & Answer Keys/ Audio CD
Listening	Listening Season 1,2,3 [1st Edition]		Student Book/ Workbook/ Scripts & Answer Keys/ MP3 CD
Listening	Listening Season 1,2,3 [2nd Edition]		Student Book/ Workbook/ Scripts & Answer Keys/ MultiROM
Listening	Listening Planner 1,2,3		Student Book/ Workbook/ Scripts & Answer Keys/ MP3 CD
Writing	Write Right Beginner 1,2,3		Student Book/ Workbook
Writing	Write Right 1,2,3		Student Book/ Workbook
Writing	Write Right Paragraph to Essay 1,2,3		Student Book/ Workbook
Speaking	Everyone, Speak! Kids 1,2,3		Student Book/ Workbook/ MultiROM
Speaking	Everyone, Speak! Beginner 1,2,3		Student Book/ Workbook/ MultiROM
Speaking	Everyone, Speak! 1,2,3		Student Book/ Workbook/ MultiROM
Grammar	Grammar Space Kids 1,2,3		Student Book/ Workbook
Grammar	Grammar Space Beginner 1,2,3		Student Book/ Workbook
Grammar	Grammar Space 1,2,3		Student Book/ Workbook
Grammar	Grammar in Mind 1,2,3		Student Book/ Workbook
Grammar	Grammar in Focus 1,2,3		Student Book/ Workbook/ Audio CD
Grammar	Grammar Effect 1,2,3		Student Book/ Workbook